T

Th

1 2 1 1 6 1 23

Mother Eva Doyle

Teaching African and African American History In the Home, School, and Community

Teaching African and African American History In the Home, School, and Community

My Journey of 45 Years

Dr. Eva M. Doyle

Library of Congress Control Number:		2023920838
ISBN:	Softcover	979-8-3694-1037-0
	eBook	979-8-3694-1036-3

Print information available on the last page.

Rev. date: 11/27/2023

To order additional copies of this book, contact:
Xlibris
844-714-8691
www.Xlibris.com
Orders@Xlibris.com
855127

CONTENTS

DEDICATION/ ACKNOWLEDGMENTS

I must thank God first for the inspiration and strength to write this book. I would like to thank my parents, James and Gertrude Townsend for insisting that I get an education and work hard to succeed. To my aunt Fannie Ruth Felts thank you for sharing our family history and your encouraging words. I dedicate this book also to my Late mother-in-law, Mother Essie Doyle, whose faith was a guiding force in my life. I dedicate this book to my Late husband Romeo Doyle Muhammad, who encouraged me to write and continue to do the research on African and African American history. He told me to keep on writing when I was ready to give up. A special thank you to Alnisa Banks who first published my newspaper column "Eye On History." In the Buffalo Challenger. It continues today in the Criterion newspaper, the oldest Black newspaper in Western New York thanks to the Late Frank E. Merriweather and his wife Evelyn

Merriweather, publishers and owners of the Criterion newspaper.

The column Eye On History will be forty-five years old in February, 2024. It has never missed a week being published in Western New York. It is my hope that this book will inspire students, educators, parents, and others to learn more about the contributions of African Americans to the nation and the world. I dedicate this book to my children, grandchildren and great-grandchildren. To my former students educators, parents, and all people who love history, it is my hope that this book will serve as a guide and inspiration to share this history in as many ways as possible. To God be the glory for this exciting opportunity to once again publish a book with history in mind.

BIO FOR DR. EVA M. DOYLE

Eva M. Doyle is a retired Buffalo Public School teacher with 30 years classroom experience. She received a Master's Degree in Elementary Education. She also studied at Capella University toward a Doctoral Degree in Educational Leadership. She received an Honorable Doctorate Degree in Humane Letters during the 148th graduation ceremony of Buffalo State College. She lectures and writes extensively on African and African American History throughout the Western New York community. Mrs. Doyle is a Columnist for the oldest Black Newspaper in Western New York – the Buffalo Criterion. Her column Eye on History is now over 45 years old. It began in the Challenger and has been published in the Buffalo News and in several national newspapers including the Chicago Defender, Today's African American Chronicle, The Palm Beach Gazette, Rochester Commicade, and Class Magazine. Dr. Doyle has written thousands of articles on African and African American history. She has also been the host of her own radio show called Eye On History for 14 years at the only Black owned and operated radio station in Western New York,

WUFO 1080. Dr. Doyle served as past Vice-President of Print of the Buffalo Association of Black Journalists (BABJ) and has served as the Vice President of print for several years. She has appeared on CNN, MSNBC and NPR discussing the Tops Massacre that occurred in Buffalo, New York on May 14, 2022. She has also appeared on panel discussions in the local media discussing the Tops Massacre where ten innocent African Americans were killed and three were injured by a white racist supremist killer. Dr. Doyle was also interviewed by ABC news for a special on the Tops Massacre. She was a guest on radio program in Los Angeles, called "Before You Go" discussing the Tops Massacre. On the first anniversary of the Tops shooting, Dr. Doyle encouraged the citizens of Buffalo to join her in turning on their porch lights in memory of the victims of the May 14th massacre. She continues to remember these innocent victims of this massacre by writing articles and doing interviews on this horrendous shooting of innocent people of the Buffalo community. Mrs. Doyle published her 12th book called Eye On History in November, 2021. It is now available on Amazon.com. Her Eye on History Billboards can be seen around the city of Buffalo. The Billboards feature outstanding African Americans in a variety of fields. Dr. Doyle has received numerous awards for her work including being named New York State Distinguished Woman of the Year by State Senator Tim Kennedy and honored by New York Assemblewoman Crystal D. Peoples-Stokes. Dr. Doyle also received the prestigious Red Jacket Award from the Buffalo History Museum. She recently received a Community Service Award from the No More Tears Organization, an organization that supports victims of homicides.

In 2010, Mrs. Doyle ran for Lt. Governor of New York State on the Freedom Party Line. Mrs. Doyle is featured on the Freedom Wall in Buffalo among 28 Civil Rights leaders. The auditorium at the Merriweather Library has been named "The Dr. Eva M. Doyle auditorium." She has done more than 100 programs in this auditorium for students, parents and the general community on African American history and education. Mrs. Doyle has introduced over 100 Essay Contests for our youth and adults. Dr. Doyle created the Roses for Outstanding Women Awards and honored over 380 women for their outstanding contributions to our community. Each woman was presented with a rose and certificates from city and state officials. She is proud of being the Founder of the Romeo Doyle Muhammad Scholarship named in honor of her Late husband, a Veteran of the Korean War. Every year she presents Scholarships to students of color who will attend college in the fall. On July 8, 2023, she gave Scholarships to six outstanding students at the 14th Annual Romeo Doyle Muhammad Scholarship Program. This award is always presented during the birth month of her late husband. Mrs. Doyle is the mother of three children, grandmother of seven, and great-grandmother of six. Dr. Doyle is also featured in a book called, "Dear Kamala" where dozens of women wrote letters of encouragement to Vice-President Kamala Harris. She was most recently honored by the Community Action Organization in the African American Heritage Banner Program as a contributing member of Buffalo. These banners surround the Dr. Martin Luther King Jr. Park in recognition of those featured for their community service. Dr. Doyle's motto is: "Learning is a Lifelong Process."

THE QUEEN AT THE LIBRARY

In honor of Queen Mother Doyle
By Taharka Odinga

Give us the Queen at the library

Fast moving Ms. Doyle

Mother of our dignity

Champion of our past

Lieutenant of our freedom

Independent truth pusher

   Keep it moving

Lights beaming all down the boulevard

Smooth and steady and serious

Summoning soldier sisters to step it up

Gracefully defiant with a Thelanious Monk

   Straight no chaser spirit

Historical sharp-shooter

Torpedoing rapid-fire at racist and lies with pristine bullets

    Read, read, read, read!

Yes the sons and daughters standing in line

Conscious Mother and Fathers

    Praying that they hit the school lottery

So that their children could have a chance

    To have real teacher in a real classroom

A faithful companion, a faithful companion, a faithful companion

Til' death do us part

RIP Brother Romeo

And the Million Man March don't stop

When the Queen Mother says rise

Dead souls get up

And inspired souls become reinvigorated 33 times

Open thine eyes, open thine eyes

Open thine eyes wide

Don't miss Ms. Doyle in action because

The Queen Mother moves fast!

INTRODUCTION

I have been researching, writing, and sharing African and African American history in numerous ways. I survived two strokes in less than four years. Despite this health scare I continue to do this work. I consider writing this book an important project while I am still here. I want to leave as much of my work as possible for my grandchildren and great-grandchildren. A local filmmaker in Buffalo named Sandy White is doing a documentary on my life. If the film comes out before this book, then it will add much to my lifelong work as an educator, and researcher and journalist. My youngest sister passed away on August 2, 2023 eight days before her birthday. I have lost two sisters in less than two years. My brother passed away in 2013. My brother Benjamin was a Veteran of the Vietnam War. My sister Leona was a devoted church member. My last sister Betty Jean worked in the healthcare field for many years. I am the last sibling of four. In three years, I will be 80 years old. My goal is to write as much as possible before this birthday. I have a lot to tell about my life and dreams. I feel that these stories must be told as I continue to go on into the future. As a student in elementary, high school, and college I did not learn much about the contributions of African Americans to our nation and to the world. I was born in Niagara Falls, New York and attended my first grade there. My father worked in a steel plant for many years. He and my mother migrated to the north in that great migration of African Americans seeking a better life. He decided to move us to Buffalo, New York in the early 1960s. He continued to work in the steel plant commuting back and forth on the Grand Island bridges between Buffalo and Niagara Falls. He worked shift work at the plant in the old coke ovens often burning himself in the hot coals. Many blacks from the south worked in the old steel plants. However, they took good care of their families. At first, we lived on the westside of Buffalo in a large apartment house on the corner of Rhode Island and Chenango in area where most of the population was Italian and Irish. My siblings and I were among the first African American students to attend school #38. Most of my classmates and teachers were white.

My sister Leona and I used to skate around the block on Richmond Avenue. The houses were huge. We thought only rich white people lived in them. Sometimes as we skated around the block, we would hear the "N" word hurled at us. We were kids and didn't understand the meaning of the word. We were just having fun like most kids. My sister Betty Jean years later told me that when she was in Kindergarten during naptime the teacher moved her to the corner of the room away from the white children and she had to sleep alone. She never forgot this experience. This memory stayed with her until adulthood. My mother went to school to complain about it. However, I never found out what happened. During these early days I was not introduced to any African American history.

My mother took us south to visit her family every summer in Alabama. My mother had seven sisters and two brothers. On those trips south we had the opportunity to get to know our aunts. We spent the whole summer on my grandfather's farm. As I look back over this experience, I realize that this was an education that we could not get in any school. We traveled by train going down to the old Central terminal in Buffalo where hundreds of African Americans waited for the trains south to visit family. This was the time of segregation. My mother packed a huge trunk and we could not wait to get on the train. We took a train called "the Humingbird." It was called that because it went faster than the other trains. I remember seeing the redcaps, the blacks dressed in red coats and white shirts carrying the luggage of white passengers. When we crossed the

Mason - Dixon line and we went deeper into the south, we were transferred to a train called "the wagon." It was a much slower train. Blacks could not eat in the restaurants or stay in the hotels. I remember seeing the white only and colored only signs along the way. My mother packed a lunch in a shoebox with fried chicken, cornbread and pound cake. It was probably better than any food in a restaurant.

Staying on my grandfather's farm for an entire summer was an exciting adventure. My grandfather, James Felts was a self-sufficient farmer. He grew everything he needed. He worked hard to make a living and take care of his family. The local community called him "Jim." He was well-known and respected. Even though he lived during the time of segregation and Jim Crow laws, he got along with others. He was willing to help others who needed help. He raised his children on the farm and taught them the value of hard work. I still remember the crops he grew. He had cows, horses, and there was a well in the front yard. I had the chance to see him milk the cows. The milk was sweet and warm, right from the cow Pasteur to the table for dinner. He grew all kinds of vegetables. There was a pecan tree in the front yard. This was the first time that I learned that peanuts grew underground. He also grew cotton, and we had the chance to try and pick cotton. It was not easy to do. There was a fig tree on the side of the house. As children we helped to feed the chickens with corn outside in the yard. We played in the sand in front of the house. There was a big swing on the front porch and we loved to sit on it.

As an adult I realize that this was an education that I couldn't get in any school room. However, there is one thing that I want to share that also has influenced me in my work today. In high school I had a teacher named Ms. Foley. She taught American History. Although, she did not teach about the contributions of African Americans she gave me an overview of this country's history. I realize that in order to understand African American history you must know the history of this country. You can see where our history fits in the important events of America. I also had a teacher named Ms. Marie Wendling. She taught us the work of the great American poets like Carl Sanberg, Robert Frost, Edgar Allen Poe and others. I was not introduced to the work of African American authors. However, these lessons taught me to appreciate poetry. Later, through my own research I learned about Langston Hughes and other great Black writers. As you turn the pages of this book it is my hope that you will see how it all fits into the general history of America. My goal is to give examples of what I did to share this history in various means.

I have studied the work of the great scholars that came before me who did research on the contributions of African people to the world. Men like Dr. Carter Woodson, Dr. W.E.B. Dubois, Dr. Chancellor Williams, Dr. Asa G. Hilliard, and others like Elleni Tedla in her book Sankofa gave me the foundation to do this work. I strongly adhere to the principal of Sankofa, a Kiswahili word that means to "go back and fetch, the history, traditions, and culture, and to go forward using it to teach and to remember." The words of Frederick Douglass, Malcolm X, Dr. Martin Luther King, Jr., have given me courage to write and to share what I know. They have inspired me in every aspect of my life. The words of the great orator Frederick Douglass ring true today when he said the following in a speech in July 5, 1852. He stated, "We have to do with the past only as we can make it useful to this present and to the future. To all aspiring motives, to noble deeds which can be gained from the past, we are welcome. But now is the time, the important time. Your fathers have lived, died, and you must do your work."

As a journalist I interviewed a number of famous people which I wrote about in my newspaper column Eye On History. The interview that I will never forget is the one I did with the wife of Malcolm X, Dr. Betty Shabazz. I interviewed her in Buffalo during a conference that was held for women at the Buffalo Convention Center in 1989. I was invited to attend the conference to cover it for the Buffalo Criterion newspaper. The organization called Women for Human Rights and Dignity, Inc. held this conference calling attention to the state of Black women. The program host, Mrs. Constance Eve, a well-known educator and community leader invited me to attend. The guest speaker was Dr. Betty Shabazz. When I walked into the Buffalo Convention Center on Saturday, April 8, 1989, I had no idea that ten minutes later I would be sitting across from the wife of Malcolm X doing an interview. I was the only journalist in the room. I asked her several questions. One of the them was: Dr. Shabazz, what message do you try to get across today to Black youth that would speak to the tradition of Malcolm X ? Dr. Shabazz answered in the following way: "I would tell them that they come from a long line of people of who built civilization. And coming from this great history of people who did so much for world civilization, they have a responsibility to accept the challenge to learn, and to help others to move forward. Being mindful of this, they must learn as much as possible. They must reconnect and recapture their heritage." The words of Dr. Betty Shabazz still ring true today and they motivate me to recapture that heritage. The chapters of this book will be a testament to the spirit of Sankofa. They will take you on a journey where the contributions of African Americans were shared through countless activities in the Buffalo community and beyond.

CHAPTER 1

The Research

Many people who read my articles want to know where do I get my research on the little known facts of African American History. I always told my students that when you write or speak on history you have to make sure that you do the research so that you can inform your audience where you went to do your research. I have used many sources of information. Here in Buffalo, we have an excellent library. The Buffalo and Erie County Public library system is a good source of information on many topics. When I first started writing my column Eye On History, I learned about the history that was not introduced in the public school system. With each article I learned something new. I used the rare book room at the library where I discovered books, tapes, old newspapers, and a file of little- known information. In order for you to use the rare book room you have to show your identification and use the materials in the library. The microfilm containing various articles in old newspapers was very useful. Many libraries might have a resource such as this one. It is something that you can check out. We have a library here in Buffalo called the Frank E.

Merriweather Library named for the publisher of the Criterion newspaper, the oldest black newspaper in Western New York. This library is the center of a variety of resources, books, tapes, films on the contributions of African Americans. There are lectures here from prominent Black authors and historians. I spend a great deal of time here. Here I have lectured, shown films, and organized programs for youth and adults.

I also used the stack room at the central library where books written decades ago can be found. Here I found old books, magazines, and other materials that helped me with my research. These books also have to be used in the library. Having the title and author can save time. I also found an encyclopedia of African American History with information on people, places and events in Black History. Doing research takes time and patience. It all pays off in the end. The librarians were very helpful and knowledgeable about the resources in the library. They assisted me greatly. Once when I was invited to speak at the Buffalo History Museum on the life of the Honorable Shirley A. Chisholm. I discovered a series of tapes in the rare book room of the library that really gave an insight into her life. Shirley Chisholm made history in Congress by becoming the first Black woman elected to the United States Congress. On November 5, 1968 she was elected to the 91st Congress from Brooklyn. She was the first Black woman to run for president of the United States in 1972. Her book, Unbought and Unbossed told the story of her life in politics. She lived in Western New York and is buried here in the Forest Lawn Cemetery. She taught at Buffalo State College. The tapes I listened to shed light on the history of Black women in law, business, education, and so many other areas. These tapes helped me to prepare for my lecture and I was able to share a lot about Shirley Chisholm the audience.

My other source of information came from the Buffalo History Museum where I spent time researching in the museum library. The museum also has exhibits on African American History. Here I found books and articles helpful to me in my research. I was also asked to lecture on the history of African Americans soldiers in the War of 1812. I found information on this topic at the research museum. It helped to write my first book called, "Buffalo's Black Community." Since Buffalo and Western New York is a very important site on the Underground Railroad where fugitive slaves came on their way to freedom in Canada. Articles on the early history of Buffalo can be found in the museum.

The Negro History Bulletin: A Good Source Of History

The Negro History Bulletin which was established in 1915 and published by the Association For the Study Of Negro Life and History, is still a good source of history. I have several copies of some of the early publications and they provide some very good information. I see these books on a regular basis and when I first started writing the column, "Eye On History" in 1979, they were a valuable resource for me. Today I still refer to them.

They contain information about Black History that you might not be able to find in a book. Some of our best sources are old, discarded materials that people look at as being obsolete. But these old books contain information that you must look high and low for today. So I treasure these books and I will always use them.

The Negro History Bulletin is filled with articles that give interesting and often little known information about our history. I have read such articles as Joel A. Rogers: An African American Historian; The Black King Who Saved Jerusalem; Paul Lawrence Dunbar; Black Poet In History; The Story of Thomas Jefferson and His Relationship With the Black Woman Named Sally Hemmings; The Black Man And The Sea; Black Explorers Of Africa, and many more.

This becomes even more important when you realize that so many African Americans have not been introduced to these books and so many others. Today, we find that there are a number of new books available. The sad thing is that we still find so many people in our community who are not aware of them. We need to introduce these materials on a wider scale. It is up to each one of us to seek out information and to share with others. If you find something good, then tell someone.

Let's save these old books and pass them on, especially to our youth. When children want to know more about the great singers such as Mahalia Jackson or Marian Anderson, I bring in their music to share with them. I had a student last year who wanted to do some research on Mahalia Jackson and write a report on her, for a class project. This student had never heard of Mahalia Jackson. So I brought in some pictures of her and a tape that showed her singing the Gospel songs that she made famous. This student was able to write her report with more feeling after seeing Mahalia Jackson and hearing her sing.

There is so much that we can do to make history come alive for our students. We can certainly begin by creating our own libraries at home. Keep the old books, because they may contain some valuable information that you can treasure for a long time.

This is an article from the Eye on History Column in 2000.

SANKOFA

The work that I have done for the past 45 years is based on the principle of Sankofa. Sankofa means to go back to the past and fetch the history, culture, and traditions in order to build for the future. Sankofa is one of the Adinkra symbols from the Akan people of West Africa. There are hundreds of Adinkra symbols. Many have various meanings. One of the most popular symbols is Sankofa that tells us that we should learn from the past. History best rewards those who do the research. The activities and projects in the pages ahead are examples of my work that carry this principle into every aspect in the community, school and home. The Sankofa bird is used to represent this spirit of reaching back. In the symbol, there is a bird looking back in the direction of its tail. Looking backwards is a quest to look to the past for a knowledge of self. In seeking knowledge an individual is attempting to find what is missing from his or her identity. This is the idea of going back to fetch it. Sankofa brings back that which is missing or lost. In these pages my quest was not only to use this idea, but in doing so, share what I have found with others. Every activity found here is based on sharing with the general community.

This sharing takes many forms such as lectures, exhibits,

films, books, performances, and all projects that will inform as many people as possible of the history and contributions of Africans and African Americans to the country and the world. By doing this hopefully it will build a better understanding between people everywhere. The negative stereotypes of people of color have existed for too long. It is not only for people of color that this book is written. It is for the wider population also.

SYMBOL OF THE WISDOM OF LEARNING FROM
THE PAST TO BUILD FOR THE FUTURE

CHAPTER 2

The Classroom Connection

In 1994 I created the first Resource Center of its kind in the public school system. The African American Resource Center was designed to assist classroom teachers in planning activities on African American history. The center provided books, posters, teaching guides, videos African artifacts, arts, and musical instruments. These, materials were available for teachers to borrow and use in their classrooms. There were also learning kits on various topics in African American history. The topics of these kits includes African storytelling, Kwanzaa, Juneteenth, the Underground Railroad, famous Black women, and the civil rights movement and Dr. martin Luther King, Jr. The goals of the African Resource included the following:

> To assist classroom teachers in planning classroom activities on the contributions of African Americans.

> To provide class presentations on various topics that included inviting guest speakers.

To encourage participation from people throughout the community.

To arrange assemble programs, create classroom projects, and hall displays.

To provide information on current issues relating to African Americans both locally and internationally.

To encourage students to write about important people in African American history through the use of writing contests.

The African American Resource Center was a mini-museum. When people walked into the room they were greeted by numerous exhibits, pictures, African artwork, and numerous wall displays. There were books on various topics from grade levels. There were materials on the role of Blacks in the civil war and the Revolutionary War. A multi-media kit was available for teachers to borrow that contained films on great events in history.

Every year we had a grand opening to introduce teachers at all grade levels to the Resource Center. The schedule of events for the year included Kwanzaa presentations in December, the Dr. Luther King assembly in January, Community Leader Day in February, and National Women's History Month in March. African American leaders from the community were invited to the school to speak to students about their careers. They represented individuals from law, business, health, education, art, and the media. We had police officers, artists, jewelry makers, judges, social workers, carpenters, and many more.

The African American Resource was in operation from 1994 to 2004 when I retired. I did have a teacher assistant who helped me in the Center. However, there was no formal plan to keep the Center active. The Center served not only the immediate school population but also the student teachers who were assigned to the school. They had the opportunity to learn how to integrate African American History in the school curriculum. A number of the professors came and brought their students into the center. I was able to do presentations on African American History and on how to use the materials available. This was a great opportunity to teach future teachers. The Resource Center was fully supported by the principal and the Board of Education. The African American Resource Center can be used by any school who would like to provide materials to teachers in their classroom. The overall goal is to help out teachers.

Additional activities from the African American Resource Center

Several students from grades 2 through 3 did presentation for guests. The presentations were designed to show how the Center enhanced student learning. The students demonstrated counting in Kiswahili. The Center introduced classes to languages spoken in Africa. The students also sang a song using these words. The other only languages introduced to our students were Spanish, French and Chinese. There was a Chinese instructor. This was an experiment in our school. However, many students had trouble learning the language. They were more successful with the other languages named here. Kiswahili was familiar to many students because it was used in the African American holiday called Kwanzaa. It was used to name the symbols and principles of kwanzaa.

Kwanzaa is a major holiday celebrated in the African American community. As a result, there were workshops for the teacher to introduce them to this holiday which is celebrated from December 26th through January 1st of each year. I invited storytellers from the community to come in and share information about Kwanzaa with our teachers. This was important to do because so many of our teachers did not know about it and in some cases were teaching incorrect information about this holiday. One of the things needed to be corrected was that kwanzaa was not a Black Christmas. Rather it was holiday celebrating the culture and traditions of African Americans. A Kwanzaa table was set up in the Resource Center that explained the symbols and the seven principals of the Holiday. I did presentations on Kwanzaa in classrooms showing how the people celebrated the holiday. Our school also introduced other holidays from various ethnic groups in order to create a better understanding of different cultures.

CHAPTER 3

The Community Connection

My journey teaching African American History continues with activities in the community. One of my missions has been to teach Black History in as many places as possible. It has taken me into a number of nursing homes to speak to seniors. One of the interesting things about speaking to our seniors is that they truly get engaged in the conversation. It is a conversation and not a lecture. They interact by giving their own experiences in life. Once I was talking about life in the south and some of the seniors told about their own lives. They shared how things were years ago with specific examples. It was a learning experience for me to hear the seniors speak. Now that I am a senior I appreciate this even more because I have my own stories to tell. A friend of mine a well-known storyteller named Karima Amin always says, "We are all storytellers." I cannot agree with her more. This is true for all races of people. When speaking to the seniors, I always listen intently and give them their space to speak if they desire to do so.

I have always brought films for them to see with various topics on African American history. They love the music videos featuring singers from past. They sing along with the songs that they know. Sometimes I have music instruments that they can play such as the shakere a music instrument that can be used like a tambourine. The picture that follows shows me in a nearby nursing home that I visited regularly. The aides would bring in the seniors, some in wheelchairs, to hear the program. This was done during the Black History Month celebrations. In this picture I am speaking about Black inventors. On the table before me are inventions by Black inventors. The ironing board was invented by Sarah Boone, a Black inventor.

Dr. Doyle presented here in a local nursing home during
Black History Month with a display showing Black inventions.

Teaching African American history with Dolls

As an educator I am always looking for ways to teach African American History. I am a doll collector. I used my dolls to introduce history to students. Adults also like to see the dolls and hear the explanation of why they are important. I have dozens of dolls all dressed in colorful attire. They have been part of my exhibits in classrooms, churches, and the local library. These dolls represent people from the past and present. They each tell a story. The picture on the following page shows an exhibit that I did for my church in celebration of Women's History Month several years ago. Some of the people that the dolls represent are Madame C. J. Walker dressed in red velvet and white fur. Madame Walker was the first African American millionaire in America. Her story is interesting because she went from poverty to creating hair care products for Black women and organizing a company to sell them employing thousands of women. She built an expensive mansion in New

York called Villa Lewaro. Her story is an inspiration to all women regardless of color.

Many of the dolls featured are dressed in African attire. The Ndebele women of South Africa have also been featured. These women are known for their unique and colorful bead work, murals. and house painting. They use bright colors and geometric shapes to create beautiful patterns on the walls of their homes. In this picture former president Barack Obama and former first lady Michelle Obama are featured. The Obama doll is a talking doll that includes a speech by the president. There is a Mandela doll also that also gives words from Nelson Mandela, the first Black president of South Africa. I gave many of the dolls African names. This is an opportunity to teach children a language that they have not heard before. This has been a very popular exhibit for all who have seen it.

A Black Doll Exhibit at the First Shiloh Baptist
Church during Women's History Month.

A WALKING CLASSROOM

I taught African History this summer at the following locations: The African American Cultural Center, the Masten Park Center, Westminster Community Canter and the Kenfield-Langfield Community Center. I would like to thank Agnes Bain, Director of the African American Cultural Center and Alesia Banner, Associate Director, for arranging for me to teach in these centers this summer.

I worked with many students from the kindergarten level to high school age. As I traveled to each of these centers, I often felt and looked like a "walking classroom". As an experienced classroom teacher, I know that in order for lessons to come alive and have a lasting impact on students, it is important to have a variety of materials and resources to use.

On my journey around the city to teach African History, I carried with me three bags filled with teaching materials to help children get a better understanding of the history and culture of African Americans. My bags were filled to capacity with books, pictures, videos, musical instruments and many other items. The following is a list of some of the materials that I carried with me:

1. The Peters Project Map. It is my feeling that you cannot begin a lesson about Africa, without introducing students to this map, because it shows the size of the continents with more accuracy than the regular maps that are used in classrooms. The idea that I want to get across to students is that Africa is the <u>second</u> largest continent in the world. I also have students define the word continent because many of them refer to Africa, as a country.

2. Books. Books. Books. I carry a wide variety of books with me as I teach African History. I do the same thing in my regular classroom during the school year. I constantly introduce new books to my students. One of the first books that I introduced this summer was a book called: "Africa Is Not A Country", written by Dr. Arthur Lewin. Another book that I use is "Egypt Is In Africa". This is an activity and coloring book by Historian Obadele Williams. This is an extremely popular book with every child that I meet. It shows Egyptian rulers who look African and includes historical information about each one. I also introduce a series of Black History comic books that tell the story of Harriet Tubman, Frederick Douglass and many others. I have dozens of issues of the American Legacy Magazine. I often give these away to students so they can take them home and share with their families. With younger students, I do lessons on animals in Africa, because I have found that many children can only identify animals such as the elephant, the lion, monkeys, snakes, etc. so in order to show them

that there are so many other animals, I use a video from National Geographic, called Swinging Safari. This is an excellent video, because it shows the famous Serengeti Plain in Africa.

The video begins with a map of Africa and goes from there. It is popular with children because it includes upbeat songs such as "Young Thing", "Lion Song", "Stripes", and "The Heart That Beats In Africa". Another popular book that I use is "Africa: Land Of the Great Cats". With older students, I introduce numerous Black scholars such as: Dr. Asa Hilliard, Dr. John Henrik Clark, Dr. Carter G. Woodson, Dr. Anthony T. Browder and many others. Books. Books. Books. I have hundreds and hundreds of books.

3. When I use videos, I always do follow up discussions and plan activities after the video so students can get a better understanding of the concepts presented. I use such videos as: The African Burial Ground In New York City, The Discovery Of King Tut's Tomb. I want to compliment Doug Ruffin, on putting together an excellent video on King Tut's Tomb. The students really enjoy it and they learn so much from it. I have dozens and dozens of videos on African History.

4. African Musical Intruments: I take with me variety of instruments such as the African Drum; the shake-a-ray, an African thumb piano; and the rain stick. I recently purchased an instrument from Kenya, called a Kayamba. I have the students play these instruments as

we sing songs of Africa. This is a hand-on activity and children love it.

5. I always take the African Liberation Flag – the red, black and green. The Honorable Marcus Mosiah Garvey, gave us this flag. I teach students about Marcus Garvey and the meaning of the flag.

6. Posters. Posters. Posters. I have hundreds of posters. I have a whole set of posters that show African Kings and Queens, and descriptions of their contributions. I have Civil Rights posters featuring African Artwork, and posters on just about any subject in African and African American History that you can think of.

7. Dolls. I use Dolls dressed in traditional African clothing, for students to learn about Africa. I have collected several dolls and I plan to purchase more this year.

8. I use hundreds of Black History worksheets to help students learn more about Africa. Anthony T. Browder's book, "Nile Valley Contributions To Civilization", comes with a beautiful workbook for students to use.

Here I am at a local high school in the cafeteria at lunchtime for students showing materials related to African and African American history. This exhibit includes books, posters, African instruments and a dvd player showing a Black history film. The students are having lunch. The assistant principle asks them to lower the noise and they really do it. They are invited to come to the table in small groups and I give them information about the things on the table. Everything is done in soft tones. The students are interested in the exhibit. The African instruments displayed include a Kora and a Shekere. The Kora is an African musical instrument that is widely used in West Africa. It has 21 strings which are played by plucking the fingers. It is built from a gourd, cut in half and covered with cow skin to make a resonator with a long wood neck. The sound of a kora resembles that of a harp. The Kora is played by skilled musicians who come from the Jali families who are traditional historians, genealogists, and storytellers. They pass their skills onto to their descendants.

The Shekere is percussion instrument from the countries of Nigeria, Benin, and Togo. The Shekere consists of of a dried gourd with beads or cowries shells woven into a net covering the gourd. It is hit against the hands to make musical sounds. I am holding a thumb piano. The thumb piano comes in many shapes some larger than others. This is just an example to show students who get a chance to not only hear the sounds but to play them as well. The goal of these lessons is to give students things that they can see, touch, and feel. As an educator it is my feeling that all lessons do not have to be held in a traditional classroom. The goal is to get students motivated to learn in an many ways as possible. When I walked into a school, I usually had a suitcase filled with learning materials. I purchased the instruments at festivals such as Juneteenth to use with students.

Dr. Doyle doing a presentation with
pictures and African instruments.

TAKING BLACK HISTORY TO A NEW LEVEL

One of my strategies in sharing the contributions of African Americans to our nation and to the world is to use Billboards. These Eye On History Billboards feature famous African Americans and give information about my community lectures on this topic. They have been seen around the community for more than 10 years in various areas in the city and beyond. They encourage people to learn more about African American History. The individuals on these Billboards include people from civil rights, politics, business, education, sports, and the military. They have featured the following:

Dr. Martin Luther King, Jr. civil rights leader

Malcolm X freedom fighter

Madame C. J. Walker, first Black millionaire

Honorable Marcus Mosiah Garvey, advocate for Black

Independence

Mary McLeod Bethune, Educator

Frederick Douglass, freedom fighter

Harriet Tubman, leader on the Underground Railroad

Isaac Murphy, Black Jockey in the Kentucky Derby

Crispus Attucks, first to die in the American Revolution

Queen Nzinga, African queen who fought for the Liberation of her people from slavery.

Dr. Carter G. Woodson, the Father of Black History

Barack Obama, first Black President of America

This is a Billboard in honor of Malcolm X and
the Honorable Marcus Mosiah Garvey.

Books for History

From time to time, individuals have asked me for a book list on topics in African and African American History. One good place to visit is the North Jefferson Library, located on Jefferson and East Utica. The North Jefferson Library contains a wealth of books for anyone interested in learning more about African History. The following are some books that contain excellent information. The author is included after each title/

Black Man Of the Nile, Yosefben Johannan.
Before the Mayflower, Levone Bennett.
Black Patriot An Martyr, Toussaint of Haiti, Ann Griffiths.
They Came Before Columbus, Ivan Van Sertima.
American Negro Slave Revolts, Herbert Aptheker.
The Life And Times of Frederick Douglass, written by Frederick Douglass.
The People Could Fly, Virginia Hamilton.
Reconstruction After The Civil War, John Hope Franklin.
Eyes on the Prize (Video And Book).
The Amistad Mutiny, Bernice Kohn.
Great Negroes Past and Present, Russell Adams.

The Trouble They Seen: Black People Tell the Story of
Reconstructions, Dorothy Sterling.
A Pictorial History Of Black Americans, Langston Hughes.
Don't Ride The Bus On Monday, (The Story of Rosa
Parks) – Louise Meriwether.
African Roots In Britain, Mekada J. Alleyne.
Marcus Mosiah Garvey: Up You Mighty People, You Can
Accomplish What You Will, Charles Barron.

The books listed here are just a few of the thousands of
books available that will open the door to African and African
American History. In addition to books, there is an increasing
variety of video and audio tapes available with topics in African
History. There is no excuse for people in this day and time not
to have some knowledge about African and African American
History. It does take time. It does take effort. However, it is
certainly worth it.

The next step is to share these books and information with
other people. This includes family members and friends. Each
one must teach another person. This will be a start toward
educating the entire community.

The North Jefferson has been replaced. A new library
was built in 2006 and the name was changed to the Frank
Merriweather Library. It was named after the publisher of the
Criterion newspaper. This library is the center of material on
African and African History in Buffalo, New York.

CHAPTER 4

Writing To Learn

One of my goals as a teacher was to encourage students to improve their writing skills. Writing should be an integral part of the classroom instruction daily on every subject. Students should experience journal writing, written responses to literature, poetry, letter writing, critiques of all kinds, research and report writing. My strategy was to use writing contests to encourage students to learn more about African American History. In this part of the book examples are given for teachers to use in their classrooms. Helping students become proficient writers is an exciting challenge for many teachers. Professional writers know that the most exciting event is that part of the writing process called publishing. Writing is an art form. A writer is like an artist who shapes, forms, develops and creates from a blank page. I have used writing contests to help students do research, think about issues, express their opinions on a variety of topics. Through the use of writing contests, students can interact with the community with their ideas.

One of the problems in education is that students don't succeed in many academic areas because they fail to see the connection between what they learn in the classroom to real life situations. Students need to know that writers can have a tremendous impact on society. They can sway opinions, raise controversial issues, provoke thought, affect politics or the economy, create new ideas or entertain. Writers tell us how to do just about everything. Writing can help to ease the stress and strain of life. I heard someone say that "writing saves lives." I have come to believe that. One of the goals of this section is to give examples of writing contests. I have introduced over 100 essay contests to help students learn more about African American history.

EYE ON HISTORY:

The History of the Eye On History Essay Contests

This Columnist has introduced Essay Contests for the past 25 years. These contests give people an opportunity to express their opinions on a wide variety of issues. When I first began to introduce them to the community the goal was to include our youth in grades 4-12 and a few times at the Kindergarten through first and second grade level. I did this for a number of years. I have introduced more than <u>100</u> essay contests. While teaching in the public schools for 30 years I made them part of my Language Arts program. Some of them were mandatory and students had to work for a grade in English. The two that were mandatory included the annual Dr. Carter G. Woodson essay contest and the annual Councilmember for a Day Contest. I had winners in each of these contests. Every year there were several students to win in each category. I also introduced the Marcus Garvey essay contest. Students had to do research on the life of the Honorable Marcus Mosiah Garvey and write an essay describing his achievements. I found that writing was one way to get them involved in learning more about African American History. Several of the students were also on my radio and television program reading their essays on the public access channel.

The following are several of the essay contests from past years. This list will give my readers some idea of the topics covered. This is just a partial list:

Councilmember for a Day, 1996. In this contest the students had to imagine that they were Councilmember for a Day and give ideas on how they would improve their community. The winners actually sat in the seat of their Councilmember at City Hall for part of the morning. This contest was sponsored by the Buffalo Common Council and the Buffalo Board of Education.

The Dr. Martin Luther King, Jr. essay contest for students in grades 4-12 was held in 2013. There were several additional contests on the topic of Dr. Martin Luther King, Jr. over the years.

A Mother's Day essay contest held in 2013 and several additional years for students. The theme was: The Best Mom in the USA. Students had to give reasons why they selected their mom for this honor.

The Earth Day Essay and Poster contest was held for

several years during the month of April for students in grades 4-12.

The Builders of the Community essay contest was held in 2014. In this contest students had to describe how they would create buildings to replace the empty lots in the city of Buffalo.

The Filmmaker essay contest, 2015. Students had to describe a film that they would like to make in Buffalo. I came up with this idea because Buffalo has become a place where filmmakers come to make movies.

The Holiday essay contest. I introduced this one several times both for youth and adults. Participants had to describe their favorite holiday and for the adults they had to describe their favorite toy that they received at Christmas as a child.

I also introduced the Dr. Martin Luther King, Jr. Speaking Contest several times for students and adults. Participants had to memorize and recite one of Dr. King's speeches.

These are just a few of my past essay contests. I have more coming in the future. Many people look forward to them and the topics presented. My latest essay contest is the $50 Million Dollar essay contest where participants had to tell how they would spend this amount of money on the East Side of Buffalo.

I had several contests and the winners were announced in the Criterion and on Facebook. The award program was held at the Merriweather Library on Saturday 11, 2019. The winners read their essays and received their prizes.

EYE ON HISTORY:

The Annual Eye On History Dressing Up for Black History Contest

The Annual Dressing Up for Black History Contest will be held

In a few weeks. I will announce the exact date in my next column. I wanted to give the information now so that perspective participants can begin to prepare for it because time is going quickly. This contest is open to high school students in grades 9-12. Students must select a person from Black History, dress up as that person, and do a 5-8 minute presentation of the person's accomplishments. This contest will be held at the Frank E. Merriweather Library located at 1324 Jefferson Avenue. The contest will be judged on creativity, oral presentation, and historical accuracy. Students must adhere to the following guidelines:

.....All presentations must be <u>memorized</u>. There will be judges in the audience and the students will lose points if they do not memorize their selections. Students will receive points on each of the areas listed above.

.....Students must dress up and select some attire that will represent the individual they are portraying. This will also be part of the point system.

.....Students must do the research to make sure that they are portraying correct history.

.....All participants must sign in at least a half hour before the program begins. This is very important so that there is no interruption of the program. In the past students have arrived at the end or in the middle of the program. This is unfair to those who come on time.

.....To get the greatest number of points it is important to follow all of the above rules.

The prizes for the winners are: First Place $100, Second Place $75, and 3rd Place $50. The names of the winners will be announced in the Criterion and on my Facebook Page and other media including the Eye On History Radio Show.

A New Essay Contest Designed for Youth and Adults

Topic: Lessons from the Life of John Lewis and Rev. C.T. Vivian

Contest Deadline: August 29, 2020

Participants must address the following in two typed pages:

1. Why was Congressman John Lewis important to the civil rights movement?
2. Describe at least two marches that he was involved in during the civil rights era.
3. Rev. C.T. Vivian was one of the leaders in the 1960s in the struggle for civil rights. Describe his role in the movement.
4. Compare the Black Lives Matter Movement to the civil rights movement of the 1960s. How is it the same? How is it different?
5. There is a move in Buffalo to designate a street with the words: Black Lives Matter. What street do you believe should be selected? Explain Why?

The prizes are $75 first place, $50 second place, and $25 third place. Participants must address all of the above. You must put your name, phone number and address on the essay!! Essays must be neatly typed. Winners will be announced on the Eye On History Radio Show hosted by Eva Doyle. You can call (716) 847-6010 for more information. This contest is sponsored by Retired Teacher Eva M. Doyle.

A Juneteenth Essay Contest

Students in grades 4-12 are invited to write an Essay on the history of the Juneteenth Celebration. The Deadline for entering the Contest is June 10, 2021. The following are the <u>rules</u> of the contest:

1. Students must give the history of Juneteenth in their essay. Why is it called Juneteenth?
2. Describe why you feel African Americans should celebrate Juneteenth.
3. Do you think that Juneteenth should be a legal holiday in all states? Why or Why not?
4. Name some of the states where it is a legal holiday.
5. How can you celebrate Juneteenth at home or in your community?
6. Please Include the following. Attach a drawing to your essay that would illustrate important parts of Juneteenth or your favorite scenes from the festival. You can use crayons or markers in your drawing. The drawing should be 8 x 10 in size. This is a <u>required</u> part of your essay, call (716) 847-6010 for more information.

Prizes are first prize $75, second prize $50, third prize $25. This Contest is sponsored by Retired Teacher Eva M. Doyle,

CHAPTER 5

The First Book

I wrote my first book called, "Buffalo's Black Community" in 1982. It will be 41 years old in February. The next section will feature the reasons why the book was published. It has been reprinted several times due to requests from many people in the community. I originally wrote it as a children's book. However, adults told me that the information in the book about the history of our community was new to them. As a result, the book has been sold to adults at many of our outdoors festivals where I have been a vendor. I gave away copies to teachers and others who wanted to use book in their classrooms. Teachers on all grade levels found it to be helpful to introduce students to the history of Buffalo and the part that African Americans played in its development. My students related to it because many of the places in the book were familiar to them. For example, some of them lived around the streets mentioned in the book. Jefferson avenue is a main street in the Black community. Yet, few people knew its history.

Although the book is 20 pages long, it took six months to do the research. Much of the research was done at the Buffalo

and Erie County Historical Society. Today it is known as the
Buffalo History Museum. There was no book on Black history
in Buffalo. This was the first book. In the years that followed
Several books and articles have been written on the history
of Blacks in Buffalo. This was a lesson for me because this
information was not in the curriculum when I was a student
in school. There is still more to do. It is my hope that future
authors will write books on this topic. The following page is
the cover of the book. It includes my three children when they
were younger. They have passed this book on to their families.

The cover of my first book published in 1982.

Eye On History:

The Book "Buffalo's Black Community"

I published my first book in 1982, 40 years ago!! The title is of it is "Buffalo's Black Community." This was the book that started me on my journey of learning more about local African American History. I would like to Al Vaughters, Channel 4 Consumer Affairs Reporter for interviewing me on Tuesday, January 25, 2022 at the Frank E. Merriweather Library for an upcoming Black History program. One of the segments on the interview centered around my first book. You will be able to see this interview in a few weeks during Black History Month in February. The date and time will be announced in the near future. We discussed a number of events in local Black History. I used Buffalo's Black Community as a starting point of our discussion.

I wrote this book when I was teaching first and second grade students in the same classroom at the Campus West School. It was during the time that Buffalo was observing its history since it was incorporated into a city in 1832. I wanted to read a book to my students that highlighted the history of African Americans in Buffalo and Western New York. I visited our school library to see if I could find a book on this topic. Unfortunately, there was no book on Blacks in Buffalo. I shared this with my Late husband, Romeo Doyle Muhammad, and he encouraged me to write my own book. This was my first time writing a book, so I did not know how to begin. One evening I sat at the dining room table with several blank sheets of typing paper. I began to make notes about what I wanted to do. I realized then that I did not really know anything about the history of Blacks in Buffalo. I decided to visit the Buffalo and Erie County Historical Society that was across the street from Buffalo State College where I taught at Campus West.

I was referred to the library at the Historical Society. They did not have a book on the contributions of Blacks in the city of Buffalo. However, what they did have were folders with articles on the African American Community. Here I found what I was looking for to use in my book. I made notes and tried to put the information in some kind of order. I also found a publication that listed the Late John Young, as the Chicken Wing King of Buffalo. It was a small notation with a picture of him at the top. There was also some information about the Black sailors who fought in the War of 1812. I had to really put everything together. What I eventually came up with was a 20-page book and I called it "Buffalo's Black Community." It took me six months to write this book.

The following information was included in the book:

1. Joseph Hodge was the first Black man to settle in Buffalo in the 1700s. He married a Seneca woman and owned a

fur trading business. He was able to speak the language of the Senecas fluently and was helpful to the early white settlers as an interpreter. He also owned the first tavern in Buffalo. He was called "Black Joe."

2. Jefferson was once called "Pollard Street" and it was the home to the German community.

3. At the end Jefferson, there was once a park called Luna Park. There was also a major carnival held there in the summer. A fire destroyed the area in 1909.

4. Black workers helped Joseph Ellicott lay out the streets in what is today downtown Buffalo.

5. Two members of famous Black families in Buffalo went to California during the gold rush and returned to Buffalo to purchase a great deal of property. They were William Talbert and Benjamin Taylor. They were wealthy landowners. I found out a few years ago that Will Talbert purchased a lot of land in Grand Island.

6. Black sailors fought bravely with Commodore Oliver Hazard Perry at the battle of Lake Erie in September, 1813.

7. I also included in the beginning of the book that there was a Black owned supermarket on Jefferson called FIGMOS, PTL. which stood for: Finally, I Got My Own Supermarket, Praise the Lord.

8. I also identified 1490 Jefferson as a major place that provided services to the Black community.

The cover of the book features my three adult children when they were still in grade school. They are Jesse Doyle, Sharif

Doyle, and Sharon Doyle. The artwork for the book was done by the Langston Hughes Institute Graphics Art Department. The artists included Cecil Von Stepp, today known as "Baba Isa", Joseph S. Capuana and Diane Dubose. The Executive Director of the Langston Hughes Institute at the time was the Late Ora Lee Delgado. It was located at 25 High Street.

I have learned a great deal since that time. This was my very first book. I plan to write an updated version of "Buffalo's Black Community." There will much more information about the history of Blacks in Buffalo. It is my goal to write the book by this summer. Writing a book is <u>not</u> easy. It requires a great deal of time and patience. When you write about history, you must do your research. I am glad that I had the experience of writing this first book because I learned a great deal!!

CHAPTER 6

Legends and Legacies

One of the things I did in my journey of teaching African American History was to create a program called "Legends and Legacies." This was a film series shown at our local library. My collections of Black History films covered numerous topics on the achievements of African Americans in politics, civil rights, business, invention, education, the media, arts, and community activism. The topics for these topics included: the lives of Harriet Tubman, Frederick Douglass, Sojourner Truth, Madame C. J. Walker, Mary McCleod Bethune, the Honorable Marcus Mosiah Garvey, Shirley A. Chisholm, Marva Collins, Malcolm X, Dr. Martin Luther King, Jr., Adam Clayton Powell.

The following are some of the titles of films I have collected:

Driving While Black, Race, Space, and Mobility in America.

Selma, Lords, Selma.

500 Hundreds Later, A Chronicle of the struggle for the freedom of African Americans.

Buffalo Soldiers, the story of Black soldiers in the West.

The Rise of the Black Pharoahs.

Dr. Frances Cress-Welsing, Racism, and Mental Health.

Ruby Bridges, a brave little girl who integrated a school in New Orleans.

Nile Valley Civilizations, narrated by Historian Anthony T. Browder.

These films also include Black entertainers such as the stars of Motown, Blues, Rock, Gospel, Reggae, and the impact on America.

Ten Things You Should Know
About African America History

They include the following topics:

The Haitians who fought in the American Revolution

The African Roots of Beethoven

U.S. Presidents of Color

The African Origin of the Statue of Liberty

The Black Woman Who Lived in the Lincoln White House

Blacks who Fought in the War of 1812.

The Black Family on the Titanic

Blacks in the Gold Rush

Black Cowboys on the Old West

Blacks in the Railroad Industry

This section can be used in classroom discussions giving students examples of the history that has been left out of textbooks.

This goes beyond Black History Month in February. It carries on the tradition of Dr. Carter G. Woodson, who was known as the "Father of Black History". Dr. Woodson saw that the accomplishments of African Americans were left out of American History. He believed that Black achievements had to be taught for a greater understanding by both Black and White races in America. He started at the time in 1926, Negro History Week. Through research he found out that African Americans had a great past. The message of Dr. Woodson still holds true today. This book is a celebration of that history.

EYE ON HISTORY:

Haitians Fought in the American Revolution

There has been a great deal of negative news recently about immigrants. However, what most people miss is the fact that immigrants from various countries have contributed in positive ways to our country. As we get closer to the July 4th holiday the role of Haitians should be recognized in the struggle for this country to become free of British rule. It may surprise some, but Haitian fighters from Haiti fought side by side with the white colonists in the American Revolution. There is a Haitian Memorial Monument honoring Haitians who fought in this war in Savannah, Georgia. They fought in a battle known as the Siege of Savannah on October 9, 1779. According to the Savannah News, the bronze soldiers on this monument represent the service and sacrifice of the Haitian Unit that fought in the siege. The hatless drummer boy is the 12 year-old future King of Haiti –– Henri Christophe.

The sculptor of this monument was James Mastin of Miami, Florida. There were two unveilings. The first one showed only four statues. But due to a single donor, the second one was unveiled in 2009 with six statues. The location of the Haitian

Memorial is in Franklin Square in Savannah, Georgia. The Haitian Unit was known as the Chasseurs-Volontaires. The Savannah Morning News reported that it was the largest unit of soldiers of African descent in the American Revolution. There was a second unit of Haitians that fought in Pensacola, Florida in 1780.

How Black Was Beethoven?

An article written by Elmer E. Wells entitled, "Beethoven and His Negroid Characteristics" provides some interesting observations about this great composer. The question to be considered here is: How Black was Beethoven? Richard Specht in a book written in 1933 entitled, "Beethoven As he Lived," wrote the following description of him, "He is a sullen being, his face is of darkish brown, like that of a Mulatto, a shock of obstinate black hair...They say his name is Beethoven." R.H. Schauffler described him as the man with the "blackish brown complexion." Friedrich Hertz stated that Beethoven was a man with coal black hair, dark eyes and dark skin.

When J.A. Rogers wrote about the Negroid traits of Beethoven, some people were very upset and many became extremely angry. It was unthinkable to them that such a powerful man of music would have any relation to Blacks.

Blacks rejected this idea from Rogers. However, when people saw Beethoven in person they referred to him as the

"Blackamoor". The word Moor or Blackmoor was used in the countries of Western Europe to describe Black people. In Germany the word was Mohr. In France the word for Black was Maure or Mohr. In Sweden it was Morian.

SEVERAL MEN OF COLOR HAVE SERVED AS U.S. PRESIDENTS

Joel Augustus Rogers wrote a book called, "The Five Negro Presidents" in 1966. This book provided evidence that all past presidents had partial Black ancestry. He identified four of the four presidents in his book. They were Warren G. Harding, Thomas Jefferson, Andrew Jackson, and Abraham Lincoln. Rogers did not identify the fifth president due to the lack of documentation at that time saying in his book that, "There seems to be no published evidence of his ancestry." Dr. Leroy Vaughn, a leading authority on Black History noted that when people called on Harding to live up to his black ancestry, Harding said that, "How should I know whether or not one of my ancestors might have jumped the fence?" This referred to the African tradition of taking a wife. This was recorded in a 2002 book called "Black People and Their World History."

William Estabrook Chancellor wrote that Harding received his education in a school founded for fugitive slaves. His genealogical records, noted Chancellor, showed that his grandfather is described as having curly kinky hair and a dark completion. The complete title of Chancellor's book is, "Warren Gamaliel Harding, President of the United States, A Review of Facts Collected from Anthropological, Historical, and Political Researches." The book was published in 1922.

According to another author named Marsha Stewart, a descendant of Harding, the Harding children attended a school for fugitive slaves.

THE AFRICAN ORIGINS OF THE STATUE OF LIBERTY

The true story of the Statue of Liberty is not known to many people. However, it is a hidden history. The Statue was originally a symbol of freed slaves. The broken chains at its feet symbolize the release from the bondage of African slaves. The Statue of Liberty was a gift to the United States from France. There were many abolitionists in France who openly opposed slavery. One of the prominent leaders of the French anti-slavery movement was Edouard de Laboulaye, the intellectual creator of the statue. He was moved by the end of the Civil War. A sculptor named Frederic Auguste Bartholdi traveled throughout Africa, and the model he chose was that of an African woman. In 2001, the History channel did a special on the Statue of Liberty and it was acknowledged that the origins of the Statue were related to the freedom on the enslaved Africans in America. On October 28, 1886, the Statue was inaugurated in New York harbor. It was declared a public holiday.

President Grover Cleveland was present to accept this gift from France. A number of anti-slavery speeches were given by prominent members of the abolitionist movement. This was the last time that the statue of Liberty was openly associated with the freedom of the slaves. There are references to the history of the Statue of Liberty in the following references: The Journal of Negro History, Volume 18, July, 1933, pages 246-255. The Birth of a Dream, New York Post, June 17, 1986, Page 2. The 2001, History Documentary of the History of the Statue of Liberty.

Millions of immigrants have passed the Statue not knowing its full history. The key element is the mosaic tablet prominently in the left hand of the Statue. Mosiac tablets have also appeared as a symbol of the abolitionist movement in this country.

ELIZABETH KECKLEY, A FORMER SLAVE WHO LIVED IN THE LINCOLN WHITE HOUSE

In the year 2013, I took a trip with my church to visit places across the United States by bus. One of our stops was at the President Abraham Lincoln Museum in Springfield, Illinois. While taking a tour of the museum we saw an exhibit that featured the president's wife, Mary Todd Lincoln. In back of her was a statue of a Black woman. Many in the tour group wanted to know who she was. There was no sign indicating her name and her importance. I answered and said, "That is the statue of Elizabeth Keckley, a former slave who lived in the Lincoln White House for four years. She was a seamstress who made dresses for Mrs. Lincoln. Elizabeth Keckley was born a slave in February, 1818. Her mother was raped by her enslaver Colonel Burwell and Elizabeth was born as a result. As a child Elizabeth was beaten, treated harshly and raped by Burwell. She was made to take care of the Burwell's white children. One was her sister. In spite of it all, Elizabeth learned how to sew from her mother. She became very skilled at sewing.

When Mary Todd Lincoln left the White House, Elizabeth came with her and helped her through her job as a seamtress. She became very good at making clothes. Later, she opened a dress shop in Washington, D.C. She purchased her freedom with money she earned from making dresses. She also purchased the freedom of her son. Later she wrote her autobiography called, Behind the Scenes, or, Thirty Years A Slave and Four Years in the White House." Due to the fact that she revealed so much about living in the Lincoln White House, there were attempts to keep the book from being published.

BLACK SAILORS WHO FOUGHT IN THE WAR OF 1812

The history of Buffalo includes a number of African Americas sailors who fought in the War of 1812. Many of these sailors passed information on to their relatives and friends about Buffalo and its proximity to Canada. Canada was seen as the land of freedom for fugitive slaves. The history of Black seaman in the American naval service goes back to the French and Indian War. Blacks maintained a presence in the U.S. Navy throughout the early republic. Although they faced discrimination, they still exhibited great bravery during the war. At first, Commodore Oliver Hazard Perry was hesitant about using Black sailors. However, after the Battle of Lake Erie in 1813, he spoke of the bravery and good conduct of the Back sailors aboard his ship.

The Black sailors came from different parts of the country. Many of them were killed in battle or taken prisoner by the British. The son of Joseph Hodge, Buffalo's first Black settler and businessman was killed in the War of 1812. One of the African American Veterans of the War of 1812 also lived in

Buffalo. His name was Peyton Harris. He served in the 4th regiment of Booth's Georgia Militia. Another Buffalo resident named Robert "Frankie" Franklin also served in the War of 1812. There is a plaque in honor of him located in front of the Connecticut Street Armory in Buffalo. Near this location stood a log cabin, owned by him. Franklin helped to successfully repel a British invasion during the war at the first Battle of Black Rock on July 11, 1813. Franklin was killed five months later when Buffalo was burned to the ground on December 30, 1813.

The best book on the African American participation in the War of 1812 is entitled: "Among My Best Men, African Americans in the War of 1812" written by Gerald T. Alfoff. Their story can also be found in the USS Constitution Museum located in Boston, Massachusetts.

THE BLACK FAMILY ON THE TITANIC

Many people are familiar with the 1997 blockbuster movie "Titanic" starring Leonardo DiCaprio as Jack Dawson and Kate Winslet as the young love of his life, Rose. What people did not see in the movie was the presence of Blacks. There was one Black family on the ship who had second class quarters. However, they had spacious rooms with beautiful paneling and furniture. They also ate in the same dining room with the first-class passengers. This family was the Joseph Laroche family. They ate with such people as the wealthy Jacob Astor who was worth at the time 30 million dollars. Joseph Laroche was traveling with his wife Juliette who was pregnant. They also had two young daughters. Joseph Laroche was born in Haiti on May 26, 1889. He came from a powerful family of influence. His uncle, Dessalines was the President of Haiti. Joseph Laroche studied engineering in France. He spoke English and French fluently. Although he had a degree in engineering, he could not find a job due to the color of his skin. He decided to return to his country of Haiti where there were more opportunities. Originally, the couple had tickets for a ship called the La France.

But they exchanged tickets for the Titanic because children were not allowed on the La France.

On the night of April 14, 1912, the Titanic struck an iceberg. The ship only had enough lifeboats for half of the passengers. Joseph Laroche put his wife and children on lifeboat number 14. However, he went down with the ship. 1500 people died in this tragic disaster. The Laroche family is listed on the passenger list of the Titanic. Author Judith Geller wrote a book about the Titanic called, "Women and Children First." She made the following statement in the book, "It is strange that nowhere in the copious 1912 press descriptions of the ship the presence of this Black family was never mentioned." The Chicago Museum featured them 88 years after this disaster.

BLACKS IN THE CALIFORNIA GOLD RUSH

During the California gold rush from 1848 to 1860, thousands of African Americans went west in search of gold and freedom. African American miners usually worked alongside of Chinese and Latin Americans. There were some integrated mining towns. There was a place called Negro Hill that attracted many non-whites. You can read more about the history of Blacks in the gold rush in a book entitled, "Blacks in the California Gold Rush." By Rudolph M. Lapp. It was published in September, 1977. Another book of interest is called, "Fugitive Slaves in the Gold Rush: the Life and Adventures of James Williams" written by James Williams and Malcolm J. Rohrbough, published in October, 2001.

According to the PBS documentary "American Experience" whites from the south brought Black slaves into California as early as the summer of 1849. Many were illegally enslaved. They worked alongside free Blacks. Their presence led to an abolitionist movement, especially in San Francisco, Oakland, and Sacramento. An estimated one-third of Blacks were illegally enslaved in California.

Many Blacks including Black women such as Clara Brown made their way to California in search of freedom. Their story has not really been told. Many made their fortunes here and were able to free some of their family members. Even in the Colorado gold rush in 1859, Blacks made their fortunes. Aunt Clara as she was called started a laundry business for miners. She was one of the Colorado Pioneers.

In my city of Buffalo, New York, I wrote about two Black men who went to California during the gold rush and came back to purchase a great of property in a place called Grand Island. These two men were William Talbert and Benjamin Taylor. They became very wealthy in the 1800's and entered into real estate here in Buffalo in the 1800's.

THE BLACK COWBOYS
OF THE OLD WEST

When I grew up as a child the only cowboys, I saw on television were Roy Rogers, the Lone Ranger, and many others who were not Black. However, there were thousands of Black Cowboys in the West and they were never recognized. Historians such as William Loren Katz and Phillip Durham wrote about them. William Katz wrote a book called, "The Black West." Phillip Durhan wrote a book called, The Negro Cowboys. I discovered another book written by Tricia Martineau Wagner entitled, "Black Cowboys of the Old West." These books are well-researched, and they give recognition to the Black cowboys that is long overdue. Wagner's book was published in 2011.

Some of the Black cowboys who became famous included Nat Love, Bill Pickett, Isom Dart, Cherokee Bill, among others. Nat Love was born into slavery in 1854. At the age of 15 he moved to Dodge City. He became known as the most skilled cowboy of the old west. Bill Pickett was a famous rodeo performer and actor. He invented bulldogging which was a rodeo event that showed cowboys wrestling steers to the ground.

Isom Dart was a cattle driver, rancher, and roper in rodeos. He settled in northwestern Colorado. He lived from 1858 to 1900.

There were others in the west who became famous for capturing some of the most dangerous cowboys in the west. Bass Reeves was one of the first Black Deputy Marshalls in the United States. He was born into slavery in Arkansas in 1838. He was known for his detective skills and markmanship with a rifle and a revolver. One of the other U.S. marshalls shown on the old television series Gunsmoke was Matt Dillion. Bass Reeves was never mentioned. In 2012, a bronze statue was erected of Bass Reeves in Fort Smith, Arkansas.

BLACKS IN THE RAILROAD INDUSTRY

Black workers in the railroad industry is a huge topic. A book by author Theodore Kornweibel, Jr. describes this history in great detail. It is a 500-page book entitled, "Railroads in the African American Experience." It takes the reader from enslavement to Amtrak. The author examines the significant contributions of African Americans to our country. The author traveled all across the country to write this history. He recounts that the history of Blacks in the railroad industry is filled with racism and abuse. He makes note that thousands of Blacks worked for decades on the nation's railroads and their story needs to be told.

This book reminds me of my childhood when my mother who was from Alabama used to take us south to visit our grandfather's farm where she grew up. We would go down to the Central Train station in Buffalo and take the trains south. I remember this clearly. Hundreds of Blacks would travel back south to visit their relatives. We took a train called the "Humming Bird." We called it the fast train. As we got closer to our destination, we transferred to another train which we called the "Wagon" because of its slow speed. This was part of the great migration, coming to the north where the living conditions for Blacks were much better. I remember the Red Caps who used to carry the luggage of the white passengers. They were polite and respectful. However, we had to carry our own bags. When we got on the train due to segregation we had to have our own lunch since the restaurants along the way were segregated and did not serve Blacks. My mother packed a huge trunk. We stayed on my grandfather's farm the entire summer until school reopened in the fall. I remember seeing the Colored and White signs. When we crossed the Mason Dixon line, everything changed as to how we were treated.

CHAPTER 7

The following pages include some of the history of Buffalo, New York area. Buffalo was a place of Freedom for fugitive slaves due to its proximity to Canada, the land of "Canaan" which was the name used by the fugitive slaves as a land where they could live in freedom. Thousands of slaves traveled through Buffalo and the entire Western New York seeking refuge in many safe houses in the area. Then the Fugitive Slave was passed in 1850. The law made it illegal to house slaves and give them refuge. Bounty Hunters came from the south looking for escaped slaves. Places such as the Michigan Street Baptist offered safety for the slaves as they traveled through the area. The small red brick church had a basement where the slaves hid behind a wall in the bathroom. It is believed to be the last refuge for the slaves. Abolitionists such as Frederick Douglass and William Wells Brown helped slaves to freedom. Douglass visited this area often from Rochester, New York.

Douglass raised money to help the fugitive slaves. He used his newspaper the North Star to speak out against slavery. He helped hundreds flee to safety. Often when he returned home, fugitive slaves would be waiting on his doorstep. He often spoke in Buffalo against the enslavement of Black people. As an agent of the Underground Railroad Douglas spoke out against the Fugitive Slave Law of 1850. He called the Law the "Bloodhound Law" because bloodhounds were used to track fugitive slaves. A building located in Buffalo at Washington and Seneca Streets was used for the first meeting by Douglass and other abolitionists of the time. Later, Bishop William Henderson and a small congregations took care of the church. Rev Jesse Nash, Sr. was one of the leaders of the civil rights movement and served as pastor of the church for many years. There is more to tell about the Underground Railroad in Buffalo and Western New York.

EYE ON HISTORY:

Buffalo: The Route to Freedom

(Authors Note: This article is being reprinted from January 31, 2020)

The city of Buffalo and Western New York was important for fugitive slaves seeking freedom. The goal was to reach the land of "Canaan" in Canada. It was seen as a sacred land of freedom. Abolitionists hid slaves in secret rooms and passageways. Although fugitive slaves received help from others, they were not helpless. They exhibited great courage and determination in the fight for freedom. They risked beatings, death, and traveled until they were exhausted. They hid by night, walked, and sometimes traveled by wagon. The slaves were acquainted with Western New York as a result of the War of 1812. Many of them served in the war. Black sailors fought on the Battle of Lake Erie with Commodore Oliver Hazard Perry in 1813. A black man named Robert "Frankie" Franklin had a log cabin built on Niagara Street in front of the site at the Connecticut Street Amory. He also served in the War of 1812. As the black soldiers came through Buffalo, they passed the word of its proximity to Canada. After the war, many returned south and told relatives about this land of freedom.

Another well-known African American named Walter Hawkins traveled along the Erie Canal to freedom. His story is written in a book published in 1891 called, "From Slavery to a Bishop or the Life of Bishop Walter Hawkins written by Celestine Edwards. He had traveled along the Underground Railroad and arrived in 1837. One of the chapters specifically speaks of Buffalo. It describes the city as a busy commercial area in 1840. The author stated that Buffalo was a city where fugitives could find work. Hawkins found a job as a waiter. He soon discovered that blacks had no place to worship except in open fields or in houses. They were not allowed to worship with whites. Hawkins was determined to learn how to read and write. He spent evenings in study. His main goal was to learn how to read the Bible. He remained in Buffalo for about three years and during this time he built the first Methodist church for blacks in the city. Author Celestine Edwards noted the following: "By building a church for his race he gave them their first lesson in the art of government and to learn how to utilize their combined resources. He taught them that there is strength in unity." Hawkins later married and left Buffalo to join his brother in Massachusetts.

Fugitive slaves made their way along the Underground Railroad throughout Western New York. The Michigan Street Baptist Church is a well-known as a place of refuge for the slaves. However, there were safe houses everywhere. Slaves traveled through Black Rock, Batavia, Lockport, Lewiston, and

Fredonia. The Eagle House on Main Street in Williamsville was a station on the Underground Railroad. Ellicott Creek behind the Eagle House was used for fugitives to escape through the countryside. The old Benjamin Baker home in Orchard Park was also a place of refuge. The Joseph Remington home in Cattaraugus County was used also. There was a hidden trap door in the home to hide slaves. The old Court Street theater was also used. It was torn down in 1927. Frederick Douglass, the great orator and abolitionist, often visited Buffalo to speak out against enslavement. Many of his meetings were held on Washington and Seneca Street. He was joined by such abolitionists as William Lloyd Garrison who also spoke in Buffalo. Douglass launched a newspaper called the North Star in Rochester to denounce slavery. He used his home as a station on the Underground Railroad.

It is estimated that over 40,000 slaves escaped to Canada by passing through Buffalo between 1830 and 1864. Some historians point to Africans settling here even before these dates. The formation of abolitionist and anti-slavery societies as well as the presence of religious groups contributed to the success of the Underground Railroad in Buffalo and Western New York.

Reprinted from January 31, 2020
Eva M. Doyle

EYE ON HISTORY:

African Americans in Buffalo: A Story of Struggle, Change, and Achievement

The first black man to come to Buffalo was Joseph Hodge. He arrived in the late 1700's. Hodge was taken prisoner by the Senecas during the Revolutionary War era. He was released by them to the authorities at Fort Stanwix in December, 1784. Hodge then returned to the Seneca Nation. He became a hunter and fur trader. Hodge established a fur trading business and a tavern. Known as black Joe, he was very helpful to the early white settlers as a guide and interpreter. Hodge married a Seneca woman. He became fluent in the language of the Senecas. He built his home on the bank of the Buffalo Creek. His presence at Buffalo Creek was noted in a report in a counsel meeting of the Seneca Nation in 1788. One of his sons was killed in the War of 1812. The arrival of Joseph Hodge was just the beginning of a community of blacks in Buffalo that saw many changes both good and bad.

Although the population of blacks in Buffalo was small in the early years, the struggle for equal rights was constant. The Buffalo Anti-Slavery Society was formed on July 4, 1834.

In August of 1843, the National Convention of Negro People held a great convention in Buffalo. A Presbyterian preacher named Henry Highland Garnett, gave a stirring address. His speech was entitled: "Address to the Slaves of the United States of America." He called upon them to rise up and fight for their lives and liberty. The Free Soil Party held a national meeting in Buffalo on August 9, 1848. It was one of the largest political gatherings ever held in the country. The theme of this convention was "Free Soil, Free Speech, Free Labor and Free men." The National Liberty Party also held a convention in Buffalo in Lafayette Square on August 30, 1848. The members adopted a resolution calling for the abolition of slavery.

The struggle for equal rights continued in the area of education. Henry Moxley was one of the people who fought constantly for equal education for blacks. He was a fugitive slave born in Virginia in 1808. He escaped to Buffalo around 1832 and in a short time he established a barber shop and purchased property by 1870. He later owned almost three thousand dollars in property. Moxley became an activist for better education. He organized a series of meetings with prominent blacks such as Peyton Harris and Dr. Benjamin C. Taylor. They protested the inferior black Vine Street School which was located in a basement under a city market. The Vine street school was described by Frederick Douglass as "a low, damp, dark cellar better fit for an ice house." Moxley finally took his case to the State Supreme Court. It was a long fight and Moxley was defeated three times. Finally, the Buffalo Common council closed the last African school in 1880.

The struggles continued and the early 1900's saw the formation of the Niagara Movement in 1905. The emergence of black leadership made an impact with such people as Rev. Jesse Edward Nash, Mary Burnett Talbert, William Talbert, Monroe Trotter, W.E.B. Dubois, John Hope and 29 others. They were not able to get hotel accommodations in Buffalo. They traveled to the Fort Erie Beach Hotel in Ontario for their first meeting which was held from July 11 through July 13, 1905. The demands of the Niagara Movement were written in a document called the "Declaration of Principles" that condemned racial discrimination and called for equal opportunities for blacks. The Niagara Movement was the forerunner of the NAACP.

Despite the challenges, blacks prevailed in a number of areas in Buffalo. They excelled in law, business, education, the media, and the arts and sports. Many became wealthy even in the 1800's with such people as Dr. Benjamin Taylor, the first black doctor in Buffalo who struck it rich in the California gold rush. He returned to Buffalo and along with William Talbert invested heavily in real estate purchasing large areas of land on Grand Island. Black literary societies and debate clubs were formed in the early 1800's. Blacks owned hotels such as the Manhattan in 1908 and the Little Savoy in 1902. The Little Harlem hotel located at 494 Michigan avenue was a popular entertainment spot that featured such people as Billie Holiday, Dinah Washington, Cab Calloway, Frank Sinatra, Bing Crosby, Louis Armstrong and many others. A black cab company known as the Brown Bomber Fleet featured drivers dressed in leather coats and hats. It was named in honor of the great heavyweight fighter Joe Louis. Black newspapers were established such as the Criterion in 1923, the Challenger, the Buffalo American, and the Voice. The historic Colored Musician's Club continues to be a major entertainment spot for great jazz and blues.

Black History Month will never cover it all. However, it is a testament to a people who have achieved much even in the face of great odds.

CHAPTER 8

Reflections, A Final Word, the Tops Mass Shooting In Buffalo

It is my hope that teachers, School Administrators, students, and the general public will use this book as a resource to learn more about African American History. This is an opportunity to learn and share with family and friends. Use it as a conversation tool. Share ideas with each other. Do further research on the topics presented. Read a little now and more at times when you can. The photo gallery at the end of this book reflect on my activities in the community over the last 45 years. There is also a section on my family and a page in Memoriam to my parents who taught me to get an education and work hard to succeed. There is also a page in Memoriam to my three siblings who have made their transition. I am the only sibling left out of four children. I lost a brother and two sisters, one passed away in November, 2022 and the last passed away in August, 2023 a week before her birthday.

Doing this work has not always been easy. It has included sadness, pain, troubles, and a horrific racially motivated shooting in Buffalo. On May 14, 2022, a mass shooting occurred in Buffalo, New York at the Tops Supermarket located on the East Side of Buffalo located at 1275 Jefferson Avenue in an area which is predominantly African American. A white racist killer traveled more than two hours to come to the Tops Supermarket with one thought in mind and that was to kill as many Black people as possible. The shooter was 18 year-old Payton S. Gendron. He lived streamed the shooting on social media. At approximately 2:30 p.m. he fired 50 rounds of ammunition outside and inside the supermarket killing ten innocent people and wounding three. He was taken into custody and was sentenced with eleven consecutive life sentences without the possibility of parole. Federal charges are still being considered. Several of the families of the victims have sought legal help to sue social media for its role in this tragedy. This was a racially motivated crime filled with hate. The killer believed in the Great Replacement Conspiracy theory that believed blacks would replace whites. He was radicalized by hate filled social media sites from the far right. President Joseph R. Biden, Dr. Jill Biden, Vice-President Kamala Harris, and others came to Buffalo to express their outrage at this mass shooting and to show support for the community. The African American Community has suffered pain and sadness after this massacre. It brought people together from all over Western New York. The fact that the Black community has only one supermarket came painfully to light. In the first year of the massacre, people organized events to provide food and other needed items to the community. Black people themselves came together to answer the need for more resources.

This columnist always did my shopping at Tops Supermarket on Saturdays around the time of the mass shooting. I changed my schedule on the date of the shooting and decided to go to the cleaners to pick up some overdue cleaning. While at the cleaners, I heard from relatives that the shooting had occurred at Tops. They were afraid that I was at Tops. There were many other people who could have been there also because many people shopped there frequently. There could have been more deaths. It is interesting because in March I had a book signing at Tops with my 12th book called Eye On History: Articles on African American History, Lost History, Forgotten History. This was the first time that anyone had a book signing at this Tops and it went well. This was two months before the mass shooting. It was a diverse crowd who came to the book signing. I can't help wondering if the shooter was present. I will never know that. However, it is a chilling thought.

I have been interviewed by ABC News, NPR news, CNN, MSNBC, and the Buffalo News about my experience and thoughts on the Mass Shooting at Tops Supermarket.

The community observed the first-year anniversary of the Tops Massacre on May 14, 2023 with programs, prayer vigils, and other events. I wanted to do something to remember the victims of the horrendous crime with a personal tribute. I asked people to join me in turning on their porch lights in the memory of the ten people who were killed and the three injured. I have also written a number of articles in their Memory. We must never forget what happened on May 14, 2022. Ten of our best citizens were taken from us. These were people who contributed much to our community. These were people who were leaders for all of the right things that made our community better. These were people of faith who helped so many in their daily work. There is a community discussion now on what would be a fitting memorial to the victims of this mass shooting. The next few pages describe the call for the community to turn on their porch lights in memory of the victims of the Tops massacre on the first anniversary. We Must Never Forget!!

In memory of the ten Black people killed in the Tops Massacre on May 14, 2022 when innocent Black people were killed by a white supremacist killer and three were injured, Dr. Doyle led a campaign on the first anniversary of this tragedy to remember the victims of this horrific killing by asking the citizens of Buffalo to join her in turning on their porch lights in Memory of the people who were killed and the three who were injured. Dr. Doyle is shown here on her front porch. She plans to make this an annual campaign and those who do not have porch lights can use a battery- operated lantern as shown here in this photo.

EYE ON HISTORY:

Remembering the Victims of the Tops Supermarket Shooting: Lights for the Victims

Our community has been under a great cloud of sadness and pain for this entire week as a result of the brutal shootings of members of our community. They were just doing what most people do on a Saturday and that is to shop for groceries. It was a normal activity with that resulted in 10 deaths and 3 injuries of innocent people. They were grandmothers, fathers, mothers, community volunteers, and supporters of our Beloved Supermarket, the only supermarket on the East Side of Buffalo. This Columnist is calling for every household that can, to put a white light on in their front porch in memory of the victims of this horrible shooting. For the next thirteen days let's remember these individuals who lost their lives in this racist attack. I will have a special light on my front door in remembrance of these victims. Let's remember their names. Call their names and never, never forget them. The names of the ten people who lost their lives and the three people injured are as follows: SAY THEIR NAMES. THEY ARE:

Margus D. Morrison, He served as a bus aide and loved his job. He was 52 and the father of 3.

Pearl Young, 77. She ran a weekly food pantry and was a teacher Aid for the School System. She loved dancing and singing. She was a grandmother and missionary.

Deacon Heyward Patterson, 67, gave rides to residents to and from the Tops Store. He attended the State Tabernacle Church of God and Christ. He was killed while sitting in his truck.

Katherine Massey, known affectionately as Kat Massey. She was Community Activist, journalist, and an advocate for justice in our community. She wrote many articles in the Criterion, Challenger, and the Buffalo News against the illegal guns. She often spoke at the Buffalo Board of Education speaking eloquently for equity for the education of our students. Her voice was powerful and she will be missed greatly.

Ruth Whitfield, 86, mother of retired former Fire Commissioner Garnell Whitfield. He called his mother an "amazing woman." She was a beloved mother wife, and grandmother. She took care of her husband who is now in a nursing home. They were married for 68 years. According to her family she was the matriarch who guided her children and grands lovingly to success in life.

Celestine Chaney, age 65, a grandmother and a regular church goer. Her daughter Dominque called her a very sweet and caring person.

Andre MacKneil, age 53 was killed on his son's 3rd birthday. He had gone to Tops to purchase a birthday cake for his son. He did make it back alive.

Geraldine Talley, age 62 a Tops shopper who lived in Buffalo.

Roberta Drury, 32, shopped for her adoptive brother who is recovering from leukemia. Roberta was the youngest person killed.

Aaron Salter, the Tops Security Guard, a retired Buffalo Police officer considered by everyone to be a Hero. He tried to engage the shooter but was killed while firing his gun which could not penetrate the armor that the shooter wore. Officer Salter most likely saved more lives.

The following people were injured and taken to ECMC. They included: Christopher Braden, Zaire Goodman, and Jennifer Washington.

IN MEMORY OF SOME OF MY FAMILY MEMBERS WHO HAVE MADE THEIR TRANSITION.

My Parents, James and Gertrude Townsend
My mother Gertrude Townsend passed away in 1986,
My father James Townsend passed away in 1988

My sister Leona Daniels
She was a Longtime Usher in her church. She
passed away on November 5, 2022.

I am with my sister Betty Jean Townsend
She passed away on August 2, 2023.

Benjamin F. Townsend
"Gabriel"

Rest In Peace

The family of Benjamin F. Townsend would like to
acknowledge with great appreciation, the many comforting
messages, tributes, prayers and other expressions of kindness
shown to us at this time in thought and deed.

Arrangements Entrusted to:

Thomas T. Edwards Funeral Home, Inc.
995 Genesee Street
Buffalo, New York 14211
Phone: 894-4888

My brother Benjamin F. Townsend
He passed away in 2013 He was a Veteran of
the Vietnam War serving in the Air Force in the
unit known as the Strategic Air Command.

My Late husband, Romeo Doyle Muhammad, A
Veteran of the Korean War. The Romeo Doyle
Muhammad Scholarship is named in Tribute to Him.
He passed away in 2009.

TOWARD A BETTER LIFE:

The Accident: A True Story

In 1967, my Late husband, Romeo Doyle Muhammad and I were in a horrific accident on the QEW – the Queens Highway in Canada on our way to a family funeral in Detroit, Michigan. My daughter was just a baby in the fall of this year. She was with my mother at the time. In those days the Doyle family would often travel to Detroit for family funerals and weddings. My husband had just left work that day. So, we packed our bags and took to the highway. He did not have much rest after a long day at work. As we drove down the highway, our car began to swerve. I could tell that my husband was sleepy. As we drove further, a state trooper put on his lights and pulled our car over to the side of the road. He asked where we were going and then he said, "I notice that your car was swerving from lane to lane and that's why I pulled you over." Sitting on the passenger side I was not really concentrating on what was said. After a few minutes the trooper rode away and we continued down the highway. What happened next was one of the most horrible accidents that I have been in my entire life. It is one that I will never forget.

In approximately ten minutes, our car was hit by a tractor

trailer. I felt a hard jolt on my side of my car. Our car was hit so hard from the back until it rolled over into a ditch on the side of the road. The car rolled over and over. The entire time it rolled over my husband never let go of my hand. After it stopped, we managed to crawl out and ran to the highway. We looked back and the tractor trailer burst into huge flames! The driver jumped straight up almost as if he was in the air. He jumped to the ground just in time. The tractor trailer burst into flames. The state trooper who had only minutes pulled us over came to the accident. Fire trucks and ambulances also arrived. Despite this terrible accident my husband and I survived. We were interviewed by the officer. We did not go to the hospital and looking back on this accident we should have went to get examined. But we later took a bus to Detroit. We did not miss the funeral.

At the time of this accident I had only one child who was just a few months old. I often think about this accident and I can close my eyes and see the flames of the tractor trailer and see the images of our car rolling over into the ditch. This happened when cell phone cameras were not in use as they are today. I don't have pictures of this accident. But I have the memory. I often hear people talk about near death experiences. This accident was one of those moments.

In retrospect I believe that God had much more for us to do in our lives. It was also a reminder of how fragile life is and how we must not take it for granted. In this time of Thanksgiving, I can reflect on this and know that although my husband made his transition many years later, his life was not in vain. He took care of his family in many ways. He made an impact on our community by being a role model as a husband, father, and leader. As we go about our daily lives it is important to remember that we never know what is around the corner. All we can do is have faith in God and the determination to lead our lives in the best way that we can after a tragedy. In thinking this all over I am reminded of Roman 8:28: "And we know that in all things God works for the good of those who love him, who have been called according to his purpose."

Romeo Doyle Muhammad from the Korean War to
private citizen, a father, husband, and community leader.

Romeo Doyle Muhammad, a young soldier in Korea

Dr. Doyle is shown here where her books along with other
authors were buried in a Time Capsule located at Broderick
Park in Buffalo, New York. Community leaders and the
general community were invited. The Time Capsule will
be opened in 100 Years! The program was attended by
community leaders and the general community. The Park
has been renamed Freedom Park because it was here that
fugitive slaves crossed the Niagara River on their way to
Canada and Freedom. Thousands of fugitive slaves came
through Western New York on the Underground Railroad.
You can see the shores of Canada from the Park.

Dr. Doyle feels blessed and says "To God Be the Glory"
for his many Blessings to continue to do this work!

Dr. Carter G. Woodson was a scholar and historian. He is known as the "Father of Black History." He started the observance of celebrating the history of African Americans in 1926. At that time it was called Negro History Week and years later it became a month-long observance and today it is African History Month and observed in February. Dr, Woodson spent years studying the history of African Americans. In 1915, he started the Association for the Study of Negro Life and History. He chose the month of February because two people who he admired had birthdays during this month. They were Frederick Douglass and Abraham Lincoln. Dr. Doyle has been inspired by the work of Dr. Carter G. Woodson and other historians like him.